Roseate Spoonbill
Pretty in Pink

by Stephen Person

Consultant: Jerry Lorenz, PhD
Director of Research, Audubon of Florida
Tavernier Science Center
Tavernier, Florida

BEARPORT PUBLISHING

New York, New York

Credits

Cover and Title Page, © Minden Pictures/SuperStock and Canon_Bob/iStockphoto; 4T, © David Walters/Miami Herald/MCT/Newscom; 4B, © Mac Stone; 5, © Minden Pictures/SuperStock; 6, © Mac Stone; 7, © McPhoto/Blickwinkel/age fotostock; 8T, © jalovell/janthinaimages; 8B, © Joe Austin Photography/Alamy; 9T, © Minden Pictures/SuperStock; 9B, © Animals Animals/SuperStock; 10, © McPhoto/Blickwinkel/age fotostock; 11, © David Pugsley Photography; 12, © Mac Stone; 13L, © Cubo Images/SuperStock; 13R, © Angela Luzader; 14T, © Jim Zuckerman/Jaynes Gallery/Danita Delimont/Newscom; 14B, © Barry Mansell/Nature Picture Library; 15, © Mac Stone; 16, © Mac Stone; 17, © Millard H. Sharp/Photo Researchers/Getty Images; 18T, © AP Photo/Wilfredo Lee; 18B, © Stephan Rose/SuperStock; 19, © State Archives of Florida; 20, Courtesy of Everglades National Park; 21T, Courtesy of Audubon Florida Tavernier Science Center; 21B, © Minden Pictures/SuperStock; 22, © Mac Stone; 24, © NaturePL/SuperStock; 25, © Claudine Laabs; 26, © Mac Stone; 27, © Jamie Felton/Flickr/Getty Images; 28, © Millard H. Sharp/Photo Researchers/Getty Images; 29, © Mac Stone.

Publisher: Kenn Goin
Editorial Director: Adam Siegel
Creative Director: Spencer Brinker
Design: Dawn Beard Creative
Photo Researcher: Picture Perfect Professionals, LLC

Library of Congress Cataloging-in-Publication Data

Person, Stephen.
  Roseate spoonbill : pretty in pink / by Stephen Person.
    p. cm. — (America's hidden animal treasures)
  Includes bibliographical references and index.
  ISBN 978-1-61772-570-8 (library binding) — ISBN 1-61772-570-6 (library binding)
  1. Roseate spoonbill—Life cycles—Juvenile literature. I. Title.
  QL696.C585P47 2013
  598.3'4—dc23
                                2012014338

For more information, write to Bearport Publishing Company, Inc., 45 West 21st Street, Suite 3B, New York, New York 10010. Printed in the United States of America.

10 9 8 7 6 5 4 3 2 1

Contents

An Early-Morning Search

The workday starts early for **biologist** Jerry Lorenz. Long before sunrise, Jerry and his team of scientists climb into a boat and cruise into Florida Bay. Their goal is to find roseate (ROH-zee-ayt) spoonbill nests on the tiny islands that dot the bay—but it's not easy.

Jerry on the lookout for roseate spoonbills

When they come to an island, Jerry jumps out and splashes to shore. As he climbs up the beach, thick vines wrap around his legs and buzzing mosquitoes surround his head. "Most days it's sweltering hot," says Jerry. "Other days it's pouring rain, or you're shivering with cold." It's all worth it, though. The reward comes when Jerry gets a close-up look at the amazing bird he has come to see.

bill

The roseate spoonbill is named for the color of its feathers and the shape of its bill. "Roseate" means pink-colored, and "spoonbill" describes the bird's bill—which is shaped like a spoon.

The Big Reward

"To see the roseate spoonbill is really great," Jerry explains. "They are like huge flowers, with wings!" Spoonbills stand nearly three feet (.9 m) tall, with a long **wingspan** of more than four feet (1.2 m). They have skinny red legs, bright pink wings, and long white necks. They have no feathers on their greenish heads, and their eyes are a glowing red.

A close-up view of a spoonbill is worth all the hard work.

Does Jerry search for spoonbill nests just so he can see these birds? No—his real job is to count them. Jerry wants to figure out if the **population** of roseate spoonbills in Florida is rising or falling. Just over 100 years ago, these birds nearly became **extinct**. Jerry and his crew of scientists are working hard to make sure this never happens again.

With their long wings, spoonbills are powerful fliers.

Jerry Lorenz works for an **environmental** group called the Audubon Society. Audubon was founded in 1886 by people who wanted to protect spoonbills and other birds.

Warmth and Shallow Water

Florida Bay and the nearby Everglades area of southern Florida are an ideal **habitat** for the roseate spoonbill. First, this area has a warm **climate**, so the spoonbills won't get too cold. It also has many small islands as well as trees surrounded by water. These places are good **nesting sites** for spoonbills. Hungry land animals like raccoons and opossums have a hard time crossing the water to reach the birds' eggs. In addition, Florida Bay and the Everglades have areas of shallow water, which spoonbills need to catch food.

Spoonbills like to build nests on small islands like this one.

It's not easy for raccoons to reach the islands where spoonbills make their nests.

In the United States, spoonbills live not only in Florida but also along the coasts of Louisiana and Texas. Areas farther north are too cold for these birds. Spoonbills also live in **wetland** areas along the coasts of Mexico and Central America, in South America, and on many islands in the Caribbean Sea.

stork

flamingos

Roseate Spoonbills in the Wild

NORTH
AMERICA

Atlantic
Ocean

Pacific
Ocean

Mexico

Caribbean
Sea

Central
America

SOUTH
AMERICA

N
W   E
S

☐ Where roseate
spoonbills live

Spoonbills belong to a group of birds known as **wading** birds. These birds wade, or walk into shallow water, to find food. Other wading birds include flamingos, egrets, herons, and storks.

Wading for Food

Why is shallow water such an important part of a spoonbill's habitat? To feed, a spoonbill needs to be able to wade into water that is not much deeper than its knees. The bird then bends its long neck, dipping its bill beneath the water. This spoon-shaped bill may look strange, but in fact it is a highly **specialized** fish-catching tool.

nostril

The spoonbill has nostrils on top of its bill, allowing the bird to breathe while most of its bill is underwater.

With its open bill underwater, the spoonbill begins sweeping its head back and forth. This movement creates tiny **whirlpools**, which pull up small fish from the bottom of muddy water and into the spoonbill's mouth. The bill is very sensitive to touch, so the bird can feel right away when a fish is touching the inside of its mouth. The spoonbill then snaps its bill shut and swallows its **prey**.

Spoonbills feed mainly on very small fish that are less than two inches (5.1 cm) long. They also eat shrimp, snails, and insects.

Spoonbills and Friends

Roseate spoonbills don't need help catching fish, yet they feed in large groups. In fact, spoonbills are very **social** animals. They like to nest in **colonies** with many birds—sometimes thousands of them. Surprisingly, these groups include not only spoonbills, but other wading birds, too, such as herons, egrets, and storks.

Spoonbills feeding with egrets and herons in Florida Bay

Scientists believe that by feeding in large groups, wading birds help each other stay safe. While searching for food, spoonbills have their heads underwater. As a result, they can't see if any animals, such as alligators and large snakes, are sneaking up on them. If many birds are in a group, not all of them will be feeding at the same time. Some will stop once in a while to take a look around to see if there are any **predators**. If danger is near, these birds let out loud warning cries. Then all the birds can fly to safety together.

Alligators often try to sneak up on spoonbills.

This spoonbill is sleeping safely in a tree.

The spoonbill sleeps standing up, usually on just one leg. While sleeping, the bird keeps its head turned backward and tucked under its back feathers for warmth.

Parents and Teamwork

Spoonbills also rely on each other when it comes time to **breed**. Female spoonbills begin the breeding process by picking a nesting site and waiting there. A male bird will then fly up to the female, carrying sticks in its bill. The male offers the sticks to the female. She uses them to begin building a nest while the male gathers more sticks, moss, and leaves.

Male spoonbills try to impress females by bringing sticks for a nest.

A spoonbill builds a nest in the lower branches of a tree that is near water.

After the nest is finished and the birds have **mated**, the female spoonbill lays from one to four eggs. For the next three weeks, the parents take turns sitting on their eggs to keep them warm. One parent stays in the nest at all times—both to **incubate** the eggs and to watch for predators.

Roseate spoonbills usually begin to breed when they are three or four years old. A male and female will produce one **clutch** of about three eggs each year. A female will continue to lay a clutch of eggs each year for the rest of her life.

A clutch of spoonbill eggs

Young Spoonbills

Once the eggs hatch, spoonbill parents have to work even harder. The tiny chicks make whistling noises to ask for food. While one parent stays with the chicks to protect them, the other flies off to catch fish and other food. When that parent returns, it opens its bill and brings up from its stomach the food it just ate. The chicks put their heads into the parent's bill and eat.

These spoonbill chicks are only five days old. Young spoonbills are lighter in color than adults and have feathers on their heads.

At about four weeks of age, spoonbill chicks begin to walk around near their nest to exercise. The young birds are strong enough to fly by the time they are eight weeks old. Young spoonbills stay with their parents for a few more weeks as they learn to feed themselves.

When they are about three months old, young spoonbills leave their parents behind and fly off to live on their own. Young birds from the same colony often stick together as they search for new homes.

Spoonbill chicks start tiny but grow quickly—so they need lots of food. This parent is feeding its chicks.

Feathers for Sale

While spoonbills are first learning to fly, they are easy prey for powerful predators like bald eagles and peregrine falcons. The good news for spoonbills is that they don't face human hunters anymore. Back in the 1800s, however, hats with bright wading-bird feathers became very popular. Hunters shot spoonbills and sold their feathers to hat companies. Spoonbill wings were also cut off and sold as fans.

Young spoonbills need to watch out for bald eagles.

A woman wearing one of the fancy feather hats that were popular in the 1800s

So many birds were killed that by the end of the 1800s, there were almost no more **breeding pairs** of spoonbills left in all of Florida. The birds were nearly wiped out in Louisiana and Texas as well. Finally, in 1900, state governments began passing laws banning the killing of wading birds for their feathers.

This photograph from the early 1900s shows a hunter in Florida with a heron that he shot.

In the late 1800s, plume hunters could earn as much as $5 for a single roseate spoonbill.

19

Wading Bird Heroes

Although states began to pass laws that made it illegal to kill spoonbills, the birds still weren't safe. In the Florida Everglades, for example, some hunters continued shooting birds and selling their feathers. As a result, in 1900, a young **warden** named Guy Bradley was hired to stop the killings. For five years he **patrolled** the Everglades, arresting people who hunted wading birds. In 1905, however, an angry hunter shot and killed Bradley. An island in Florida Bay, close to the place where Guy Bradley was killed, is named for him.

Today, Guy Bradley is still remembered for his brave work protecting spoonbills.

Another person who has helped the spoonbill survive is an **ecologist** named Robert Porter Allen. In 1938, Allen set up a tent near a spoonbill colony on Bottle Key, a small island in Florida Bay. Spending day after day knee-deep in mud, he was the first scientist to study spoonbills up close. Much of what scientists know about these birds today comes from Allen's work.

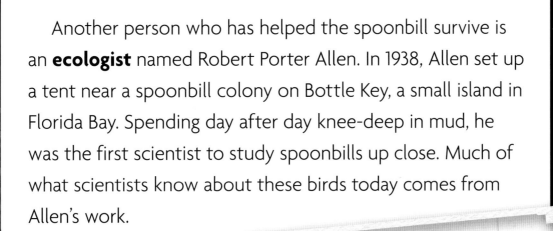

To study the spoonbill, Robert Porter Allen lived as close to their habitat as he could. Allen studied the birds for more than 35 years.

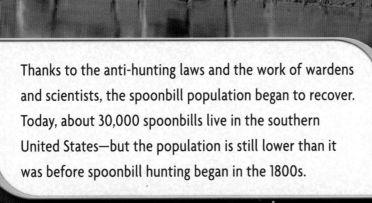

Thanks to the anti-hunting laws and the work of wardens and scientists, the spoonbill population began to recover. Today, about 30,000 spoonbills live in the southern United States—but the population is still lower than it was before spoonbill hunting began in the 1800s.

Threats Today

The spoonbill population is **stable** today, but the birds still face threats. One major problem is habitat loss. People have drained the water from many wetland areas so the land could be used for new farms or buildings. When this happens, spoonbills lose habitat they rely on for feeding and breeding.

New homes and farms have replaced more than half of the original Everglades.

In Florida, the biggest threat facing spoonbills is the way humans have changed the Everglades. Millions of people in south Florida rely on the **freshwater** that flows from Lake Okeechobee through the Everglades. The water is pumped into homes and used to **irrigate** farms. As more water is pumped out of the Everglades for people to use, less freshwater flows from the Everglades into Florida Bay. Why does this lack of freshwater hurt spoonbills?

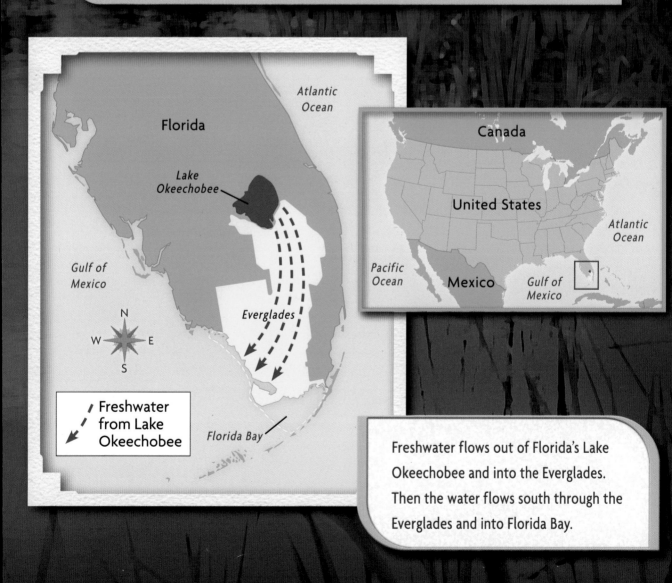

Freshwater flows out of Florida's Lake Okeechobee and into the Everglades. Then the water flows south through the Everglades and into Florida Bay.

Ecosystem at Work

The Everglades and Florida Bay form one huge **ecosystem**. The animals and plants in this community depend on one another to live. When people pump freshwater out of the Everglades, less freshwater flows into Florida Bay and the water in the bay becomes saltier. As a result, some underwater plants die because they don't grow well in salty water.

Florida Bay is home to a huge variety of plants and animals, including manatees such as this one.

When fewer plants grow, the fish that rely on these plants for food have less to eat—and some of them die. These events have a direct effect on spoonbills, because the spoonbills rely on fish as their main source of food. When spoonbill parents can't catch as many fish, chicks starve and the population falls.

By studying spoonbills like this young bird, Jerry Lorenz learns about the health of the entire ecosystem.

The spoonbill is what scientists call an **indicator species**. This means the spoonbill helps show how healthy an ecosystem is. When the spoonbill population falls, scientists know something is wrong with the entire ecosystem.

The Effort Continues

Jerry Lorenz knows that spoonbills can **thrive** only as part of a healthy ecosystem. On days they're not counting birds, Jerry and his fellow scientists paddle kayaks through the Everglades. They jump out and wade through the water, setting traps for the tiny fish that spoonbills need for food.

Jerry at work

Counting these fish is another way of studying the health of the Florida Bay and Everglades ecosystem. It's exhausting work and can even be dangerous. "One of us always stays in the boat," explains Jerry, "to watch for sharks, crocodiles, and alligators." So why do Jerry and other biologists risk their lives? Simple, says Jerry. "We're trying to do something good for spoonbills—and the entire ecosystem."

The Everglades and Florida Bay are also very important to the **economy** of south Florida. People spend billions of dollars to go boating, fishing, and diving in this beautiful area. Without a healthy ecosystem, fewer people will visit and less money will be spent.

Roseate Spoonbill Facts

The roseate spoonbill is closely related to another pink bird—the flamingo. Here are some other facts about the roseate spoonbill.

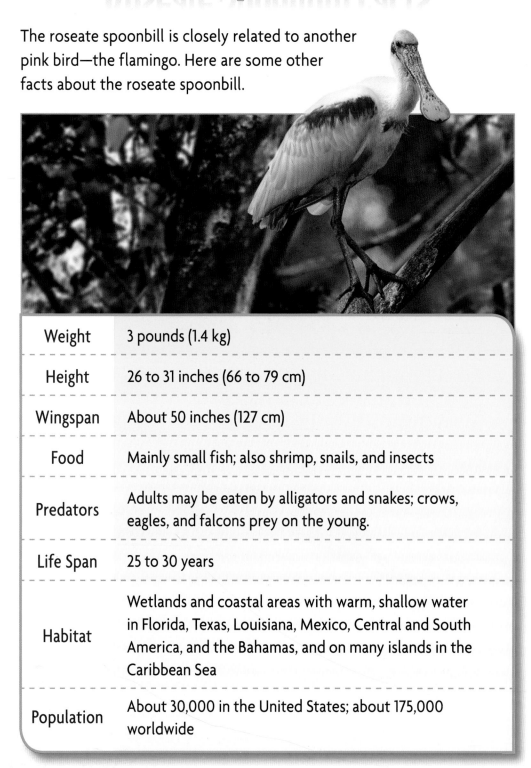

Weight	3 pounds (1.4 kg)
Height	26 to 31 inches (66 to 79 cm)
Wingspan	About 50 inches (127 cm)
Food	Mainly small fish; also shrimp, snails, and insects
Predators	Adults may be eaten by alligators and snakes; crows, eagles, and falcons prey on the young.
Life Span	25 to 30 years
Habitat	Wetlands and coastal areas with warm, shallow water in Florida, Texas, Louisiana, Mexico, Central and South America, and the Bahamas, and on many islands in the Caribbean Sea
Population	About 30,000 in the United States; about 175,000 worldwide

People Helping Spoonbills

Hunters used to be the biggest danger facing roseate spoonbills. Today, the birds are safe from hunters but face the danger of losing their habitat. Fortunately, many people are working to protect these birds and the ecosystems they depend on.

National Audubon Society

- At the Tavernier Science Center in Florida, Jerry Lorenz and his team of scientists are studying the populations of both roseate spoonbills and the fish they feed on.
- Other Audubon biologists are studying spoonbills that nest on islands in Tampa Bay, Florida.
- Audubon scientists are also working to improve the health of the Florida Bay and Everglades ecosystem.

Jerry Lorenz looking for roseate spoonbills

Everglades Foundation

- The Everglades Foundation is one of many environmental groups in Florida that are working to improve the health of the Everglades environment.
- The key to this effort is to increase the flow of clean freshwater through the Everglades.
- Another big part of the group's job is to teach people about the Everglades and the amazing variety of animals that live there.

Florida Department of Environmental Protection

- This government organization is in charge of protecting Florida's natural resources and making sure environmental laws are followed.
- The agency is working with scientists, environmental groups, and businesses to put the Everglades Restoration Plan into action. This is a 30-year plan to **restore** the steady flow of clean water into the Everglades.

Glossary

biologist (bye-OL-uh-jist) a scientist who studies plants or animals

breed (BREED) to produce young

breeding pairs (BREED-ing PAIRZ) two animals, one male and one female, that come together to breed

climate (KLYE-mit) patterns of weather over a long period of time

clutch (KLUCH) a group of eggs that a bird lays at one time

colonies (KOL-uh-neez) groups of animals that live together

ecologist (i-KOL-uh-jist) a person who studies the relationships between plants and animals, and their environments

economy (i-KON-uh-mee) financial activity

ecosystem (EE-koh-*siss*-tuhm) a community of animals and plants that depend on one another to live

environmental (in-*vye*-ruhn-MEN-tuhl) having to do with the land, air, and sea

extinct (ek-STINGKT) when a type of animal or plant completely dies out

freshwater (FRESH-*wa*-tur) water that does not contain salt

habitat (HAB-uh-*tat*) a place in nature where a plant or animal normally lives

incubate (ING-kyuh-bayt) to hatch eggs by keeping them warm

indicator species (IN-di-kay-tur SPEE-sheez) a kind of animal that helps scientists measure the health of the entire ecosystem in which it lives

irrigate (IHR-i-gayt) to supply with water

mated (MAYT-id) came together to produce babies

nesting sites (NEST-ing SITES) places where animals build nests and lay their eggs

patrolled (puh-TROHLD) traveled around an area to protect it

population (*pop*-yuh-LAY-shuhn) the number of people or animals living in a place

predators (PRED-uh-turz) animals that hunt and kill other animals for food

prey (PRAY) an animal that is hunted by another animal for food

restore (ri-STOR) to bring something back to its original condition

social (SOH-shuhl) living in groups

specialized (SPESH-uh-*lyezd*) very focused on one thing

stable (STAY-buhl) steady

thrive (THRIVE) to grow or to do well

wading (WAYD-ing) walking in or through shallow water

warden (WOR-duhn) a person whose job it is to look after protected areas and the animals that live there

wetland (WET-*land*) marshy land; land where the soil is very moist or wet

whirlpools (WURL-poolz) water that moves in a circle and can pull objects into it

wingspan (WING-*span*) the distance between the tips of a bird's wings

Bibliography

Allen, Robert Porter. *The Roseate Spoonbill*. New York: Dover (1966).

Cornell Lab of Ornithology: The Birds of North America Online/Roseate Spoonbill (http://bna.birds.cornell.edu/bna/species/490/articles/introduction)

National Audubon Society: Roseate Spoonbill (http://birds.audubon.org/species/rosspo)

National Wildlife Refuge Association: Critter Corner/Roseate Spoonbill (http://www.fundrefuges.org/critter/spoonbill.html)

Read More

Kalman, Bobbie. *Everglades National Park*. New York: Crabtree (2010).

Lynch, Wayne. *The Everglades (Our Wild World)*. Minnetonka, MN: NorthWord Books for Young Readers (2007).

Marx, Trish. *Everglades Forever: Restoring America's Great Wetland*. New York: Lee & Low Books (2004).

Miller, Sara Swan. *Wading Birds: From Herons to Hammerheads (Animals in Order)*. New York: Franklin Watts (2001).

Learn More Online

To learn more about roseate spoonbills, visit
www.bearportpublishing.com/AmericasHiddenAnimalTreasures

Index

About the Author

Stephen Person has written many children's books about history, science, and the environment. His first job after college was with the National Audubon Society, in Washington, D.C. He lives with his family in Saratoga Springs, New York.